VALUING THE PRE-OWNED VEHICLE

VALUING THE PRE-OWNED VEHICLE

Sachin A Mulge

Worldwide Published by
Pendown Press
PREMIUM BUSINESS PUBLISHER

PENDOWN PRESS LLP

An ISO 9001 & ISO 14001 Certified Co.,

Regd. Office: 3767A, Kanhaiya Nagar,

Tri Nagar, Delhi-110035

Ph.: 8130886000, 9650072927

E-mail: info@pendownpress.com

Branch Office: 1A/2A, 20, Hari Sadan, Ansari Road,

Daryaganj, New Delhi-110002

Ph.: 011-45794768

Website: PendownPress.com

First Edition: 2024

Price: ₹299/-

ISBN: 978-93-6338-322-7

Layout and Cover Designed by Pendown Graphics Team

Printed and Bound in India by Thomson Press India Ltd.

Contents

MY JOURNEY

In the vibrant streets of Mumbai, my journey began as a fresh-faced graduate in the world of automobile engineering back in 1997. Tata Motors welcomed me into their fold, where I immersed myself in the Complexities of vehicle manufacturing and testing. With each passing day, I absorbed knowledge like a sponge, laying the groundwork for what would become a fulfilling career.

The next chapter of my journey unfolded at Ford Motors' soon-to-open dealership in Mumbai. Here, I delved into the exciting realm of new-generation vehicles, witnessing the transition from traditional carburetor technology to advanced ECM-based systems. My dedication didn't go unnoticed, earning me promotions and responsibilities overseeing critical tasks like pre-delivery inspections, ensuring top-notch quality for every vehicle that left our showroom floor. Yet, my curiosity wasn't confined to new cars alone. Intrigued by the world of pre-owned vehicles, I took on a part-time role at a prominent used car dealership. In the hustle and bustle of Mumbai's pre-owned car market, I found my niche, **learning everything from** procurement to refurbishment and sales. Soon, I became a trusted name in the industry, known for my keen insights and contributions.

In the year 2000, I **started working in** insurance surveying and vehicle valuation, offering my expertise to banks and insurance companies. It wasn't long before my reputation as a seasoned expert in the pre-owned vehicle sector caught the attention of Late. Mr. Kamlesh Bulchandani, a credit manager at a prominent bank. In 2008, I was offered a pivotal role as a valuation agency—a role where I truly flourished, cementing my status as a leading figure in India's valuation landscape. Fueled by my passion for pre-owned vehicles, I delved deeper into the world of OEMs' methodologies for vehicle inspection. My dedication caught the eye of Mahindra First Choice, India's pioneering multi-brand pre-owned organized player. Impressed by my insights and expertise, they welcomed me aboard, entrusting me with inspection responsibilities on a pan-India scale. My journey with Mahindra First Choice took me far and wide across India's diverse pre-owned car market. During a particularly memorable assignment in Kolkata, my keen eye uncovered a major accident-repaired vehicle, which left a lasting impression on the management and **further solidified** my reputation as a meticulous evaluator.

Driven by a hunger for innovation, I **contributed** my expertise to various startups, helping them establish robust vehicle grading methodologies. One standout collaboration involved harnessing algorithms and cutting-edge technology to revolutionize the validation of vehicle values, pushing the boundaries of what was thought possible in the industry.

But my journey didn't stop there. I partnered with a company specializing in pre-owned vehicle warranties, using my extensive knowledge to refine warranty products tailored specifically for the Indian market. My contributions played a crucial role in crafting sophisticated warranty offerings, setting new standards and raising the bar for the industry.

Through dedication, perseverance, and an unwavering passion for automobiles, I carved out a path marked by excellence and innovation—a journey that continues to inspire and shape the future of India's pre-owned vehicle landscape.

Focus Point

- Started in 1997 at Tata and Ford Motors, gaining expertise in vehicle manufacturing and inspection.
- Built a reputation in pre-owned vehicle valuation, working with Mahindra First Choice on nationwide inspections.
- Innovated vehicle grading and warranty solutions, setting new standards in India's pre-owned vehicle market.

Chapter

01

Introduction to Used Vehicle Valuation

In the banking industry, the valuation of used vehicles is an important process for determining the collateral value of a vehicle for loan purposes. The valuation process helps banks to assess the risk of lending against a particular vehicle and determine the loan amount to be sanctioned to the borrower. Additionally, used vehicle valuation holds significance for dealerships and other businesses engaged in the sale and purchase. It aids in establishing the fair market value of a vehicle and negotiating a reasonable price with the buyer or seller.

The process of vehicle valuation involves assessing the overall condition of the vehicle, determining its market value, and establishing a fair market price. In order to determine the condition of the vehicle, the valuer would inspect the vehicle's exterior, interior, engine, and other mechanical components. The inspection would involve checking for any visible damage or signs of wear and tear, as well as reviewing the vehicle's service history and maintenance records.

After assessing the condition of the vehicle, the valuer proceeds to determine its market value by comparing it with similar vehicles presently listed for sale in the market. The valuer would consider factors such as the age, mileage, make and model of the vehicle, as well as the current market demand for the particular type of vehicle.

Upon assessing the condition and market value of the vehicle, they would provide a fair market price that takes into account the condition of the vehicle and the current market demand. The fair market price plays a crucial role in ensuring that the borrower or seller receives a reasonable value for the vehicle and that the lender or buyer is not taking on an undue risk.

In summary, the valuation of used vehicles holds great significance in the banking industry as well as in the sale and purchase of vehicles. It helps to determine the fair market value of a vehicle, assess the risk of lending against it, and negotiate a reasonable price with the buyer or seller. The process involves assessing the overall condition of the vehicle, determining its market value, and providing a fair market price based on the current market demand.

Focus Point

- **Purpose:** Used vehicle valuation helps banks assess lending risk and dealerships set fair prices.
- **Process:** Involves inspecting condition and comparing market listings
- **Outcome:** Provides a fair market price, balancing value for sellers and minimizing risk for buyers/lenders.

Chapter

02

Factors That Affect Used Vehicle Valuation

Used vehicle valuation is influenced by numerous factors that directly affect their market value. In this chapter, we will explore in-depth the factors that affect used vehicle valuation, including mileage, age, and condition of the vehicle, brand and model popularity, and the dynamics of market demand and supply. We will also provide examples to illustrate how these factors can significantly impact the valuation of a used vehicle.

Mileage, Age, and Condition of The Vehicle

Mileage, age, and condition are fundamental factors that significantly impact the valuation of a used vehicle.

Mileage: Mileage refers to the total distance traveled by the vehicle. Generally, lower mileage is desirable and indicates less wear and tear on the vehicle. Higher mileage can lead to reduced valuation, as it implies more usage and potentially higher maintenance or repair needs.

Example: Consider two identical model-year sedans, one with 50,000 kilometers (31,000 miles), while the other has covered 150,000 kilometers (93,000 miles). The vehicle with lower mileage is likely to have a higher valuation due to the perception of less wear and tear.

Age: The age of a vehicle is another crucial factor in determining its valuation. As vehicles age, they undergo normal wear and tear, and technological advancements may make older models less desirable.

Example: A 5-year-old vehicle may have a lower valuation compared to a similar model that is only 2 years old. This is primarily due to factors such as outdated technology, potential mechanical issues that can arise with age, and the perception of newer vehicles being more desirable.

Condition: The overall condition of the vehicle encompasses its physical appearance, mechanical performance, and maintenance history. Vehicles that are in excellent condition, free of significant damage, and possess a well-documented maintenance history, typically receive higher valuations.

Example: A well-maintained vehicle with no accidents or major repairs is likely to have a higher valuation compared to a similar vehicle with visible damage, signs of neglect, or a history of mechanical issues.

Brand and Model Popularity

The brand and model popularity significantly influenced vehicle valuations. Some brands and models enjoy strong market appeal and retain their value better than others.

Example: A luxury brand renowned for its reliability, performance, and strong resale value, such as a Maruti Wagon R, Hyundai i20 Series, is likely to have a higher valuation compared to a less popular brand or model with similar mileage and age. The popularity of a brand and model is influenced by factors such as reputation, market demand, and perception of quality.

Market Demand and Supply

The dynamics of market demand and supply also impact used vehicle valuations. Supply and demand fluctuations can affect the perceived value of a vehicle.

Market Demand: The demand for specific types of vehicles can vary based on consumer preferences, trends, and market conditions. Factors such as fuel efficiency, safety features, and lifestyle appeal play a pivotal role in shaping the demand for particular vehicles.

Example: In recent years, there has been a growing demand for fuel-efficient and electric vehicles due to environmental concerns and rising fuel costs. This increased demand may lead to higher valuations for these types of vehicles.

Market Supply: The availability of similar vehicles in the market can impact valuations. When there is a high supply of a particular make and model, it often results in more competitive pricing and potentially lower valuations. On the other hand, a limited supply can increase the value of a vehicle.

Example: If a specific model is in high demand but there is limited availability in the market, it may command a higher valuation due to its scarcity.

Focus Point

- **Key Valuation Factors:** Mileage, age, and vehicle condition strongly influence used vehicle valuation, with lower mileage, newer age, and better condition generally leading to higher values.
- **Brand Popularity:** Popular brands and models with high resale value, like luxury or reliable brands, tend to retain higher valuations.
- **Market Dynamics:** Demand and supply fluctuations affect valuation, with high demand or limited supply driving up prices, while oversupply may lower them.

In summary, several factors influence used vehicle valuations. Mileage, age, and condition of the vehicle play a significant role, with lower mileage and excellent condition typically leading to higher valuations.

Chapter

03

Techniques For Used Vehicle Valuation

There are several techniques that can be used to accurately determine the value of a used vehicle. In this chapter, we will discuss the three most frequently used techniques for used vehicle valuation: physical inspection and testing, comparative market analysis, and appraisal software and tools.

Physical Inspection and Testing

Physical inspection and testing is the most traditional and widely used method of valuing a used vehicle. This technique involves conducting a comprehensive visual and mechanical inspection of the vehicle to assess its current condition. The valuer would inspect the vehicle's exterior, interior, engine, transmission, and other mechanical components. Additionally, they would perform a test drive of the vehicle to evaluate its performance and handling characteristics.

During the inspection, the valuer carefully examines the vehicle's body for any indications of wear and tear, rust, dents, and scratches. They would also check the condition of the tires, brakes, suspension, steering, and other components for any signs of damage or wear. The valuer would also inspect the vehicle's documentation, including the registration certificate, insurance papers, and service history.

Physical inspection and testing is a time-consuming and labor-intensive process, yet it provides the most accurate assessment of the vehicle's current condition. It is an important technique for used vehicle valuation as it helps to identify any hidden concealed or issues that could affect the vehicle's value.

Comparative Market Analysis

Comparative market analysis involves researching the current market value of similar vehicles in the area to determine the fair market value of the vehicle being valued. This technique involves comparing the make, model, age, mileage, and condition of the vehicle being valued with similar vehicles currently listed for sale in the market.

The valuer would utilize online marketplaces, auction sites, and classified ads to gather information about similar vehicles currently available for sale. They would also take into account the demand and supply dynamics for the particular type of vehicle in the local market.

Comparative market analysis is a useful technique for used vehicle valuation as it offers a comprehensive understanding of the current market conditions and helps to identify the fair market value of the vehicle based on the current supply and demand.

Appraisal Software and Tools

Appraisal software and tools refer to computer programs and online tools designed to streamline the process of used vehicle valuation. These tools use algorithms and data analysis to calculate the fair market value of a vehicle based on various factors, such as the make, model, age, mileage, and condition of the vehicle.

Some of the most popular appraisal software and tools used for used vehicle valuation include Indian Blue Book , OBV Book. These tools are widely used by dealerships, banks, and other businesses involved in the sale and purchase of vehicles.

Appraisal software and tools are convenient and efficient, but they may not always provide an accurate valuation of the vehicle. This is because they do not consider the vehicle's specific condition and service history, which are factors that can significantly impact its value.

In summary, the three most commonly used techniques for used vehicle valuation are physical inspection and testing, comparative market analysis, and appraisal software and tools. Each technique possesses its own set of advantages and limitations, making it crucial to utilize a combination of techniques to provide an accurate valuation of the vehicle.

Example: Let's take the example of a 2016 Honda Civic with a mileage of 50,000 km, which is being evaluated for a bank loan. We will discuss how each of the three techniques for used vehicle valuation can be applied to this specific example.

Physical Inspection and Testing

The first step in the physical inspection and testing technique involves visually inspecting the vehicle's exterior, interior, engine, and other mechanical components. In this case, the valuer would inspect the Honda Civic's body for any dents, scratches, or signs of rust. They would also check the condition of the tires, brakes, suspension, steering, and other mechanical components.

During the test drive, the valuer would check the engine performance, transmission shifting, and the vehicle's handling. They would also pay attention to any unusual sounds, vibrations, or smells that might indicate a potential issue with the vehicle.

After the inspection and testing, the valuer would grade the vehicle's overall condition based on a standardized grading system. For example, they may grade the Honda Civic's condition as "Excellent," "Good," "Fair," or "Poor." The vehicle's condition grade would be used to determine its value.

Comparative Market Analysis

For the comparative market analysis technique, the valuer would conduct research on the current market value of similar Honda Civics in the local market. They would specifically focus on Honda Civics with the same model year, similar mileage, and condition to the one being valued.

The valuer would use online marketplaces, classified ads, and auction sites to gather information on similar Honda Civics currently available for sale in the market. They would also consider the demand and supply for Honda Civics in the local market.

Based on their comprehensive research, the valuer would then calculate the fair market value of the Honda Civic being valued. The fair market value would be determined by considering the average price of similar Honda Civics in the local market.

Appraisal Software and Tools

For the appraisal software and tools technique, the valuer would rely on a computer program or an online tool designed to calculate the valuation based on various factors such as the make, model, year, mileage, and condition of the vehicle. They would input the information on the Honda Civic being valued into the software or tool, and it would generate a comprehensive valuation report.

Some popular appraisal software and tools for used vehicle valuation include Indian Blue Book, Orange Blue Book, the valuer would use the valuation generated by the chosen tool to determine the fair market value of the Honda Civic accurately.

In conclusion, each technique for used vehicle valuation has its own sets of advantages and limitations. To ensure an accurate valuation of a used vehicle, a combination of these techniques is often employed. By considering the individual condition, mileage, make, and model, as well as current market demand and supply a comprehensive and precise valuation can be obtained.

Focus Point

- **Physical Inspection:** Comprehensive evaluation of a vehicle's condition through visual checks and test drives ensures accurate assessment.
- **Comparative Market Analysis:** Fair market value is determined by comparing similar vehicles in the local market.
- **Appraisal Tools:** Software-based valuations provide efficiency but lack consideration for specific physical and historical details.

Chapter

04

Common Valuation Errors and How to Avoid Them

Valuation errors can occur due to several factors such as inaccurate condition grading, failure to consider market trends, and overvaluing or undervaluing the vehicle. In this chapter, we will discuss these common valuation errors and how to avoid them.

Inaccurate Condition Grading

One of the most common valuation errors is inaccurate condition grading.

This error occurs when the valuer assigns an incorrect grade to the vehicle's overall condition. Condition grading is an important factor in used vehicle valuation as it helps to determine the vehicle's value based on its condition.

To avoid this error, the valuer should adhere to a standardized grading system and conduct a comprehensive physical inspection and testing of the vehicle. It is also advisable to consult industry-recognized appraisal guidelines such as the National Automobile Dealers Association (NADA) or the Kelley Blue Book to determine the appropriate condition grade for the vehicle.

Failing to Consider Market Trends

Another common valuation error is failing to consider current market trends when determining the value of a vehicle. Market trends such as supply and demand, seasonal fluctuations, and changes in consumer preferences can have a significant impact on a vehicle's value.

To avoid this error, the valuer should conduct research on the current market conditions and trends specific to the local area. They should consider factors such as the availability of similar vehicles, recent sales prices, and any noticeable changes in consumer preferences. By considering market trends, the valuer can provide a more accurate valuation of the vehicle.

Overvaluing or Undervaluing the Vehicle

Overvaluing or undervaluing a vehicle is another common valuation error. Overvaluing a vehicle can lead to the lender or buyer taking on an undue risk, while undervaluing a vehicle can lead to the seller receiving less than the fair market value.

To avoid this error, the valuer should use a combination of valuation techniques such as physical inspection and testing, comparative market analysis, and appraisal software and tools. By using a combination of techniques, the valuer can provide a more accurate valuation of the vehicle and avoid overvaluing or undervaluing it.

In summary, common valuation errors such as inaccurate condition grading, neglecting market trends, and overvaluing or undervaluing the vehicle can lead to inaccurate valuations and potential financial losses. By following industry-recognized appraisal guidelines, conducting a thorough physical inspection and testing of the vehicle, and considering current market trends, the valuer can avoid these common errors and deliver a precise valuation of the vehicle.

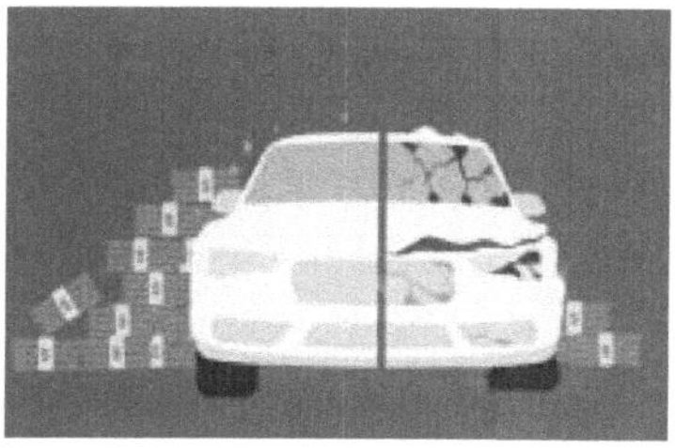

Focus Point

- **Inaccurate Condition Grading:** Avoid errors by using standardized grading systems and thorough physical inspections with industry-recognized guidelines.
- **Neglecting Market Trends:** Ensure accurate valuation by researching local market trends, including supply, demand, and consumer preferences.
- **Overvaluing or Undervaluing:** Prevent inaccuracies by combining multiple techniques, such as physical inspections, market analysis, and appraisal tools.

Chapter

05

Valuation For Different Vehicle Types

Valuation for different vehicle types involves considering the unique characteristics of each type of vehicle when determining its worth. In this chapter, we will discuss the different calculation methodologies and current market trends for three types of vehicles:

1. Passenger Cars

Passenger cars are the most common type of vehicle, and the valuation process for these vehicles involves several calculation methodologies including:

Depreciation: Depreciation is calculated based on the age and mileage of the vehicle, and it is one of the most critical factors in determining the vehicle's value. The rate of depreciation varies across different car models, underscoring the importance of considering the make, model, and year of the car when calculating depreciation.

Comparative Market Analysis: Comparative market analysis is an essential methodology used to determine the value of passenger cars. This approach involves comparing the make, model, year, and condition of the vehicle with similar vehicles currently available for sale in the market. To gather information on comparable vehicles, the valuer utilizes online marketplaces, classified ads, and auction sites.

The current market trend for passenger cars is shifting towards fuel-efficient and electric vehicles. In recent years, there has been a notable increase in demand for eco-friendly cars, leading to a surge in the popularity and demand for hybrid and electric vehicles.

2. Commercial Vehicles

Commercial vehicles include trucks, buses, and vans used for commercial purposes. The valuation process for these vehicles involves several methodologies of calculation such as:

Replacement Cost Method: This method entails calculating the cost of replacing the vehicle with a new one. Factors taken into account for determining the replacement cost include the vehicle's age, condition, and mileage. The replacement cost method is most commonly used for new commercial vehicles.

Income Method: The income method involves calculating the revenue generated by the commercial vehicle. The valuer would consider factors such as the type of vehicle, its usage, and the demand for the services it provides.

The current market trend for commercial vehicles is shifting towards electric and hybrid vehicles. Numerous countries are actively promoting the use of eco-friendly commercial vehicles by offering incentives and subsidies, leading to increased demand for these vehicles.

3. Two-wheelers

Two-wheelers include motorcycles, scooters, and mopeds. The valuation process for these vehicles involves several methodologies of calculation such as:

- **Age-Based Depreciation:** Age-based depreciation is the most commonly used methodology for valuing two-wheelers. It involves calculating the depreciation based on the age of the vehicle. The rate of depreciation varies among different models, emphasizing the importance of considering the make, model, and year of the two-wheeler when calculating depreciation.
- **Comparative Market Analysis:** Comparative market analysis is another significant methodology used for valuing two-wheelers. This involves comparing the make, model, year, and condition of the vehicle with other two-wheelers currently available for sale in the market.

The current market trend for two-wheelers is shifting towards electric and eco-friendly vehicles. Many countries are actively promoting the use of electric two-wheelers by offering incentives and subsidies, thereby fostering increased demand for these vehicles.

In summary, the valuation process for different types of vehicles involves considering the unique characteristics of each type of vehicle. The methodologies of calculation and current market trends vary for each type of vehicle, requiring a combination of techniques to ensure an accurate valuation.

Focus Point

- **Passenger Cars:** Valuation focuses on depreciation, comparative market analysis, and growing demand for fuel-efficient and electric vehicles.
- **Commercial Vehicles:** Methods include replacement cost and income-based approaches, with rising interest in eco-friendly electric and hybrid options.
- **Two-Wheelers:** Age-based depreciation and market comparisons are key, alongside increasing demand for electric and environmentally sustainable models.

Chapter

06

Regulatory Framework For Vehicle Valuation in India

The valuation of used vehicles is a crucial process for determining the collateral value of a vehicle for loan purposes. In India, the Reserve Bank of India (RBI) and Securities and Exchange Board of India (SEBI) have laid down guidelines and regulations for used vehicle valuation. In this chapter, we will discuss the regulatory framework for vehicle valuation in India, emphasizing on the RBI guidelines for used vehicle valuation for banks along with the SEBI regulations for vehicle valuation for Non-Banking Financial Companies (NBFCs).

Banks must implement a standardized methodology for used vehicle valuation, considering the factors such as the vehicle's age, mileage, make and model, and overall condition.

- Banks must appoint independent valuers to value used vehicles. The valuers must have adequate experience in vehicle valuation and must follow a standardized grading system for assessing the condition of the vehicles.

- Banks must ensure that the valuation is based on a physical inspection and testing of the vehicle. The valuer must inspect the vehicle's exterior, interior, engine, transmission, and all other mechanical components.
- Banks must ensure that the valuer considers current market trends and other relevant factors such as supply and demand for the specific type of vehicle in the local market.

An example of how these guidelines may be applied is when a bank is valuing a 2018 Maruti Suzuki Swift with a mileage of 20,000 km. The valuer would follow the RBI guidelines and employ a standardized methodology to evaluate the vehicle on the basis of its age, mileage, make and model, and overall condition. Furthermore, the valuer would conduct a physical inspection and testing of the vehicle considering the current market trends in order to provide an accurate valuation for the bank.

SEBI Regulations for Vehicle Valuation for NBFCs

SEBI has established regulations for vehicle valuation for Non-Banking Financial Companies (NBFCs) to ensure that they adopt a standardized and transparent process for valuing vehicles. The regulations are as follows:

NBFCs must appoint independent valuers to value vehicles. The valuers must possess enough experience in vehicle valuation and essentially follow a standardized grading system for condition grading.

- NBFCs must ensure that the valuation is based on a physical inspection and testing of the vehicle. The valuer must inspect the vehicle's exterior, interior, engine, transmission, and other mechanical components.
- NBFCs must ensure that the valuation is based on the current market value of the vehicle, taking into account factors such as the age, mileage, make and model, and overall condition of the vehicle.

An example of how these regulations may be applied is when an NBFC is assessing the value of a fleet of commercial vehicles. The valuer would follow the SEBI regulations and use a standardized methodology to value the vehicles based on their age, mileage, make and model, and overall condition. In addition to that, the valuer would conduct a physical inspection and testing of the vehicles and consider the current market value of the vehicles to provide an accurate valuation for the NBFC.

In summary, the guidelines and regulations of RBI and SEBI on used vehicle valuation for banks and NBFCs respectively, is to ensure that a standardized and transparent process is followed for valuing vehicles. The guidelines and regulations ensure that the valuations are accurate, transparent, and fair, thereby protecting the interests of all stakeholders involved in the valuation process.

Focus Point

- **RBI Guidelines:** Banks must follow standardized methodologies, appoint experienced independent valuers, and ensure valuations are based on thorough inspections and market trends.
- **SEBI Regulations:** NBFCs are required to adopt transparent processes, use standardized grading systems, and conduct physical inspections to ensure accurate valuations.
- **Stakeholder Protection:** Both frameworks aim to maintain fairness and transparency in vehicle valuation, safeguarding the interests of banks, NBFCs, and customers.

Chapter

07

Valuation For Loan Approvals

Valuation for loan approvals involves determining the collateral value of a vehicle for loan purposes. In this chapter, we will explore how vehicle valuation affects the loan approvals, the pros and cons of using vehicle valuation for loan approvals, and examples of how vehicle valuation affects loan amounts.

How Vehicle Valuation Impacts Loan Approvals

Vehicle valuation is a crucial factor in loan approvals, as it directly impacts the collateral value of the vehicle. The collateral value represents the maximum amount that can be borrowed against the vehicle. A higher collateral value means that the borrower can borrow a higher amount of money.

The lender will typically require a valuer to determine the collateral value of the vehicle. The valuer will use a combination of techniques such as physical inspection and testing, comparative market analysis, and appraisal software and tools to determine the fair market value of the vehicle. The fair market value is then used to decide the collateral value of the vehicle.

Pros and Cons of Using Vehicle Valuation for Loan Approvals

Pros:

— Vehicle valuation ensures that the loan amount is based on the fair market value of the vehicle, protecting the interests of both the borrower and lender.

— Vehicle valuation provides a standardized and transparent process for determining the collateral value of the vehicle.

— Vehicle valuation aids in reducing the risk of loan defaults, by providing assurance to the lender that the collateral value of the vehicle is adequate to cover the loan amount.

Cons:

— Vehicle valuation can be time-consuming and expensive, as the valuer must conduct a physical inspection and testing of the vehicle.

— Vehicle valuation can result in a lower loan amount if the fair market value of the vehicle is lower than expected.

— Vehicle valuation can result in a higher loan amount if the fair market value of the vehicle is higher than expected, leading to potential financial risks for the lender.

Examples of How Vehicle Valuation Affects Loan Amounts

- **Example 1:** A borrower wants to take a loan against a 2015 Honda City with a mileage of 60,000 km. The valuer determines that the fair market value of the vehicle is INR 500,000. Considering the lender's loan-to-value ratio of 80%, the collateral value of the vehicle is INR 400,000. Hence, the borrower is eligible to borrow a maximum loan amount of INR 400,000 against the vehicle.
- **Example 2:** A borrower intends to take a loan against a 2019 Toyota Fortuner with a mileage of 30,000 km. After conducting a valuation, the valuer determines the fair market value of the vehicle at INR 2,000,000. Based on the lender's loan-to-value ratio of 80%, the collateral value of the vehicle is determined to be INR 1,600,000. Consequently, the maximum loan amount that the borrower can borrow against the vehicle is INR 1,600,000.

In summary, vehicle valuation is an important factor in loan approvals, as it determines the collateral value of the vehicle. By using a combination of techniques, the valuer can provide an accurate valuation of the vehicle, protecting the interests of both the borrower and lender. Although there are pros and cons to using vehicle valuation for loan approvals, it remains an essential procedure for ensuring fair and transparent loan approvals.

Chapter

08

Valuation For Vehicle Sales

Valuation for vehicle sales involves determining the fair market value of a used vehicle for pricing and marketing purposes. In this chapter, we will discuss how to use valuation to determine sale price, share best practices for promoting a used vehicle, and provide examples of how valuation impacts the sales of vehicles.

How to Use Valuation to Determine Sale Price

Valuation plays a vital role in determining the sale price of a used vehicle. The fair market value of the vehicle serves as the initial reference point for determining the sale price. The valuer will use various techniques such as physical inspection and testing, comparative market analysis, and appraisal software and tools to determine the fair market value of the vehicle.

Once the fair market value has been determined, the seller can take into account additional factors such as the overall condition of the vehicle, mileage, make and model, and any additional features or upgrades. These factors can influence the final sale price of the vehicle.

Best Practices for Marketing a Used Vehicle

Marketing a used vehicle involves several best practices to attract potential buyers and ensure a successful sale. These practices include:

Creating a detailed listing: The listing should include all relevant information about the vehicle, including its make and model, year, mileage, and any additional features or upgrades. The listing should also include high-quality photos of the vehicle.

Setting a competitive price: The sale price of the vehicle should be based on its fair market value, considering factors such as its condition, mileage, and other relevant factors. The price should be competitive with other similar vehicles currently available for sale in the market.

Advertising the vehicle: The seller should advertise the vehicle on multiple platforms, including online marketplaces, social media, and classified ads to reach a wide audience of potential buyers.

Conducting a thorough inspection: Prior to listing the vehicle for sale, the seller should conduct a comprehensive inspection of the vehicle to ensure that it is in good condition. Any issues or necessary repairs should be addressed before marketing the vehicle.

Offering a test drive: The seller should offer potential buyers a test drive to allow them to experience the vehicle's performance and features.

Examples of How Valuation Affects Vehicle Sales

- **Example 1:** A seller intends to sell a 2017 Ford EcoSport with a mileage of 40,000 km. The valuer determines that the fair market value of the vehicle is INR 600,000. Considering the vehicle's condition, the seller decides to list the vehicle for sale at INR 650,000. The seller promotes the vehicle on multiple platforms and offers a test drive to potential buyers. Eventually, after negotiating, the vehicle is sold for INR 625,000.
- **Example 2:** A seller wants to sell a 2015 Honda City with a mileage of 50,000 km. The valuer determines that the fair market value of the vehicle is INR 450,000. Based on the vehicle's condition, the seller decides to list the vehicle for sale at INR 500,000. Unfortunately, the seller fails to promote the vehicle effectively and does not receive any offers for several weeks. To attract the potential buyers, the seller decides to lower the price of the vehicle to INR 475,000 and as a result of the same, the vehicle gets sold.

In summary, valuation is a critical factor in determining the sale price of a used vehicle. By using a combination of techniques, the valuer can provide an accurate valuation of the vehicle, which allows the seller to set a competitive sale price. Effective marketing practices such as creating a detailed listing, setting a competitive price, and conducting a thorough inspection can attract potential buyers and ensure a booming sale.

Chapter

09

Future of Used Vehicle Valuation

The future of used vehicle valuation is constantly transforming due to technological advancements and changes in the automotive industry. In this chapter, we will explore the emerging trends in vehicle valuation technology, the impact of electric and autonomous vehicles on used vehicle valuation, and the future of used vehicle valuation.

Trends in Vehicle Valuation Technology

Technology is rapidly transforming the way vehicles are valued. The following are some of the key trends in vehicle valuation technology:

Artificial Intelligence (AI) and Machine Learning (ML): AI and ML are being used to analyze the extensive large amounts of data to determine the fair market value of vehicles. This technology can consider various factors such as make and model, age, mileage, and condition, enabling it to deliver more precise valuation in comparison to conventional methods.

Blockchain: Blockchain technology is being used to develop a secure andtransparent system for recording vehicle valuations. This technology can help prevent fraud and ensure that the valuations are accurate and reliable.

Augmented Reality (AR) and Virtual Reality (VR): AR and VR technology are being used to create virtual inspections of vehicles. This advanced technology empowers valuers to inspect and test vehicles remotely, significantly reducing the time and cost of physical inspections.

The Impact of Electric and Autonomous Vehicles on Used Vehicle Valuation

Electric and autonomous vehicles are rapidly changing the automotive industry, and they are also influencing the valuation of used vehicle The following are some of the key ways that electric and autonomous vehicles are affecting used vehicle valuation:

Battery Life: Electric vehicles are equipped with batteries that degrade over time, and the cost of replacing them can be substantial. This can impact the resale value of electric vehicles.

Autonomous Features: The prevalence of autonomous features such as self-driving technology and advanced safety features are becoming increasingly common in vehicles. These features can affect the resale value of vehicles, as buyers may be willing to pay a higher price for vehicles equipped with advanced safety features.

- **Maintenance:** Electric and autonomous vehicles often have distinct maintenance requirements compared to traditional vehicles. Valuers will need to consider these factors when determining the fair market value of these vehicles.

The Future of Used Vehicle Valuation

The future of used vehicle valuation is likely to be shaped by technology advancements and transformative shifts in the automotive industry. Valuers must adapt to these changes to ensure the continued accuracy and reliability of their valuations. The following are some of the key trends that are likely to shape the future of used vehicle valuation:

- **Increased Use of Technology:** The use of technology such as AI, ML, and blockchain is likely to become more widespread in the valuation of used vehicles.
- **Shift to Electric and Autonomous Vehicles:** As more electric and autonomous vehicles enter the market, valuers will need to develop new methods for valuing these vehicles.
- **Focus on Sustainability:** The automotive industry is focusing more on sustainability, and this trend is likely to affect the resale value of vehicles. Valuers will need

to consider the environmental impact of vehicles while determining their fair market value.

In summary, the future of used vehicle valuation is likely to be influenced by technological advancements and shifts in the automotive industry. Valuers will need to keep up with these changes to ensure that their valuations remain accurate and reliable. Electric and autonomous vehicles are likely to have a significant impact on used vehicle valuation, and valuers will need to develop new methods for valuing these vehicles.

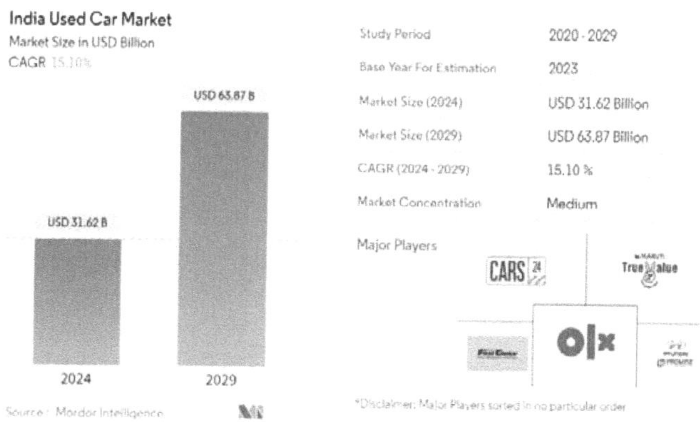

CONCLUSION

Summary: A Comprehensive Guide to Used Vehicle Valuation for Bank Credit Managers and Sales Managers

"The Comprehensive Guide to Used Vehicle Valuation for Bank Credit Managers and Sales Managers" is a comprehensive book that offers valuable insights into the world of used vehicle valuation in India. With a focus on creating authority and credibility for automobile engineers and valuers, this book strives to be a trusted resource for bank credit managers and sales managers.

The book covers various essential topics, including an introduction to used vehicle valuation, factors that affect used vehicle valuation, techniques for valuation, regulatory frameworks, and the future of the industry. It provides detailed explanations of each topic, allowing readers to gain a comprehensive understanding of the valuation process.

Readers will gain the understanding of the crucial role played by accurate vehicle valuation in the banking industry, the significance of factors such as mileage, age, and condition of the vehicle in determining its value, and the impact of market trends on valuation. The book explores various valuation techniques, including physical inspection and testing, comparative market analysis, and appraisal software and tools. It highlights the pros and cons of each technique, which equip the readers to make informed decisions in their valuation practices.

Additionally, the book explores the regulatory framework for vehicle valuation in India, providing insights into the RBI guidelines for used vehicle valuation in banks and the SEBI regulations for valuation in NBFCs. It emphasizes the significance of adhering to standardized and transparent processes to ensure fairness and accuracy in valuations.

Moreover, the book sheds light on the future of used vehicle valuation, considering emerging trends in technology and the impact of electric and autonomous vehicles on the industry. It explores the use of AI, blockchain, and AR/VR in valuation processes and discusses how the growing popularity of electric and autonomous vehicles affects valuations.

Throughout the book, readers will find real-life examples that illustrate how valuation decisions can make an impact on loan approvals, sale prices, and marketing strategies. These examples will help readers to connect theoretical knowledge with practical applications, which will enhance their understanding of the valuation process.

"The Comprehensive Guide to Used Vehicle Valuation for Bank Credit Managers and Sales Managers" serves as an authoritative resource, aiding readers in establishing their expertise in the eyes of bank managers in India. Through its valuable insights, guidelines, and illustrative examples, the book equips readers with the essential knowledge and tools required to confidently and accurately navigate the complex world of used vehicle valuation with confidence and accuracy.

CASE STUDIES

Case Study 1

Allow me to share one such tale that epitomizes the essence of our work.

It was a brisk Monday morning, the clock ticking towards 11:00 a.m., when we received a directive from a leading bank. Given our established position on their panel, we promptly scheduled an appointment with the client, aligning with their convenience, for a meticulous inspection of a vehicle. Bright and early on Tuesday, my team and I arrived at the designated location, ready to engage with the customers. Following a brief introduction, we delved into the inspection process. The vehicle in question was a premium model, boasting considerable value. However, as we began our inspection, it became evident that beneath its glossy exterior lay a hidden truth—structural damages, painstakingly concealed to mask its troubled past.

Our seasoned eyes didn't falter in recognizing the tell-tale signs of an accident-ridden history, a fact overlooked by a previous inspection agency. With precision and diligence, we conducted our assessment, meticulously documenting our findings in a comprehensive report, which we promptly submitted to the credit manager the following day.

Upon reviewing our report, the credit manager reached out to me, his tone laced with incredulity. "Sachin Ji, are you certain about these findings? How could the valuation be so significantly lower?" he asked. I patiently guided him through the detailed analysis in the report, reaffirming our assessment of the vehicle's true value in light of its accident history.

His initial skepticism quickly transformed into gratitude and admiration. "Sachin sir," he exclaimed, "you've not only revealed the true nature of this vehicle but also safeguarded our bank from substantial financial risk. Your diligence has saved us over 30 lakhs! We are immensely grateful for your expertise and dedication."

As our conversation drew to a close, he expressed his heartfelt appreciation once more, acknowledging the significance of our discovery in preserving the integrity of their operations.

In that moment, amidst the exchange of pleasantries and gratitude, it became abundantly clear—the importance of our role transcends mere transactions; it's about safeguarding trust, integrity, and the financial well-being of our partners.

Case Study 2

Once upon a time, I received a special assignment from a big bank. They wanted me to inspect a fancy Lamborghini car. The bank had some basic info about the car from the owner, but they thought the value seemed too high. So, they asked me to check it out.

Me and my team went to the place where the car was parked. When we got there, we found out the owner had looked up the car's value on a popular website called "Sales Capture." It said the car was worth a whopping 1 crore 60 lakhs! That's the same value the owner had told the bank.

But here's the thing, online values can sometimes be way off. So, we did our own inspection, looking at every detail of the car. And guess what? We found out it wasn't worth as much as the website said. It had some issues that lowered its value.

The next day, I told the bank about our findings. I explained that online values can be different from the real value you find with a hands-on inspection. With our inspection, we could tell if the car had been in an accident or had been fixed up. That's important for knowing the true value.

When I told them our valuation was only around 90 lakhs, they were surprised. They asked if I was sure. I confidently explained our methods and how we arrived at the value, especially in such a short time.

They were happy with our work. They thanked us for the detailed information and said they were satisfied with our service. They even mentioned that they had heard about me before and knew I was good at what I do. But now, they had seen it for themselves and were really pleased.

Case Study 3

Once, I had a meeting with the sales department of a bank. They were interested in adding me to their panel of experts. During the meeting, I had the opportunity to meet with both their credit team and sales team. I took the chance to introduce myself and my team, highlighting our expertise and the modern techniques we employ in our inspections.

As I explained our methods, one concern stood out: the use of pencils for taking chassis impressions. This traditional method had its limitations, especially when it came to detecting alterations. I reassured them by introducing them to the advancements in digital printing technology. With this new technology, we could digitally capture the chassis number, making it tamper-proof. Instead of relying on pencil imprints, we suggested using digital photographs that could be zoomed in to verify the authenticity of the chassis number.

Their worries eased upon learning about these technological advancements. The meeting concluded successfully, with everyone feeling satisfied.

On the day of inspection, the excitement from the bank's team was palpable. They were eager to witness our new method in action. As we proceeded with the inspection, our digital approach uncovered something alarming: two chassis numbers on the vehicle. It was evident that one was original, while the other had been tampered with.

We immediately alerted them to this fraudulent activity. Thanks to our digital method, they decided against funding the vehicle, thus averting a potential non-performing asset situation. The demonstration of our advanced techniques left them impressed.

Following the successful inspection and grading, we submitted our report to their branch. The positive feedback we received served as motivation to continually improve and excel in our work. It underscored the importance of dedication, teamwork, and the utilization of advanced techniques. These moments of professional collaboration inspire us to tackle new challenges with renewed enthusiasm, exceeding expectations every step of the way.

CALL TO ACTION

Dear Readers,

As we reach the end of this book, I would like to express my deepest gratitude for taking the time to read this book.

I'm eager to hear how "The Comprehensive Guide to Used Vehicle Valuation for Bank Credit Managers and Sales Managers" has impacted you. Your experiences can be incredibly helpful in guiding others who are also exploring this valuable resource.

If you've discovered anything insightful or have questions that others might benefit from, please share! Your input could make a big difference for someone else.

Feel free to reach out with your thoughts or inquiries at ***sachinmulge@gmail.com***. Together, we can make a difference by sharing knowledge and helping others navigate the world of vehicle valuation.

Warm Regards,

Sachin Mulge